FIVE PILLARS OF PROSPERITY

Essentials of Faith-Based Wealth Building

ABRIDGED EDITION

GIVEN TO ME BY
ABDALLA IDRIS ALI

FIVE PILLARS OF PROSPERITY

Essentials of Faith-Based Wealth Building

M. Yaqub Mirza

ABRIDGED EDITION

IIIT

LONDON • WASHINGTON

IIIT
P.O. BOX 669, HERNDON, VA 20172, USA
www.iiit.org

LONDON OFFICE
P.O. BOX 126, RICHMOND, SURREY TW9 2UD, UK
www.iiituk.com

Printed and published by permission of White Cloud Press, Ashland,
Oregon, USA, publisher of the original unabridged edition, 2014.

ISBN 978-1-56564-562-2

Cover and Typesetting by Saddiq Ali

To my parents, siblings (especially Dr. Ishaq Mirza), in-laws, children, extended family, and my beloved wife, Tanveer
also
To my brothers and sisters in Abrahamic faith and all other faiths who desire to live in peace, love, and prosperity.

General Disclaimer

The information contained in this book was obtained from various sources. The author does not guarantee its accuracy or completeness nor the accuracy or completeness of the analysis relating to it. Any party relying on the contents will be doing so at his or her own discretion.

This book is for general circulation and is provided for general information only. It should be treated as a guide and as a service to community. The information, examples, and case studies in this book are intended to be a general introduction to financial management. They are not intended to be either a specific offer by any Sterling Management Group Inc. entity or person to sell or provide, or a specific invitation to apply for, any particular product or service. Sterling Management Group Inc. and its affiliates offer a broad range of investment advisory and financial services. The nature and degree of advice and assistance provided, the fees charged, and client rights and Sterling Management Group Inc.'s obligations will differ among these services. Neither Sterling Management Group Inc. nor its personnel provide individual legal or tax advice. Clients should review any planned financial transactions and strategies that may have legal or tax implications with their personal advisors.

Although the author is a founder and trustee of Amana Mutual Funds Trust and a board member of University Islamic Financial (UIF), a subsidiary of the University Bank, the work is entirely that of the author. Neither the Trust nor its advisor, Saturna Capital Corporation, nor UIF and University Bank, suggested the creation or production of this work.

CONTENTS

FOREWORD

FIVE Pillars of Prosperity: Essentials of Faith-Based Wealth Building by Dr. Yaqub Mirza, is an important introduction and guide to Islamic finance, savings, planned spending and wealth creation. Taking an easy to understand, practical and sensible approach, the author explains to regular Muslims and readers, how to ethically and productively manage their finances and savings to improve their economic well-being both in the short term and forseeable future, equipping them to meet the challenges of all those areas that make up most of our daily and future financial affairs.

Dr. M. Yaqub Mirza has more than four decades of experience in Islamic finance and wealth management. He has been advising on Shariᶜah compliant financial transactions, and is overseeing Islamic/ethical investments involving assets close to $4 billion. He has spoken widely and published many articles on the subject and believes passionately that Muslims should understand and create a wealth management plan for themselves in accordance with their faith, needs and circumstances to secure their financial future.

In addition, he serves on the board of Shenandoah University, George Mason University Foundation, Chairman of Amana Mutual Funds, and many more. His email address is mym@sterlingmgmt.com.

Where dates are cited according to the Islamic calendar (hijrah) they are labelled AH. Otherwise they follow the Gregorian calendar and are labelled CE where necessary. Arabic words are italicised except for those which have entered common usage. Diacritical marks have been added only to those Arabic names not considered modern.

Since its establishment in 1981, the IIIT has served as a major center to facilitate serious scholarly efforts. Towards this end it has, over the decades, conducted numerous programs of research, seminars and conferences as well as publishing scholarly works specialising in the social sciences and areas of theology, which to date number more than four hundred titles in English and Arabic, many of which have been translated into other major languages.

IIIT London Office
January 2018

PREFACE

PROSPERITY has long been cherished as a goal. The desire is universal and rightly so. Prosperity is desired to provide an atmosphere congenial for living with dignity. Human beings are here on earth to demonstrate that one can be good by choice. They are to compete with one another in attaining moral excellence. That is what raised humans' stature not only above animals but also above angels, the "no sin, no wrongdoing" creatures!

In the hundred and fifty or so pages [in the unabridged edition] that follow these lines, Dr. Mirza, whom I have known as a pious people's money manager since 1972, when we first met, tells you how to go about working for prosperity. The message is simple: earn, save, invest, spend, and give. What is unique about this that justifies the writing of a book? Well, for a complete answer you have to read the book. But I can tell you something to begin with. The significance lies in the sequence. Also, each one of these five steps implies a certain mindset, rather, an ethic. Focus on these and you have your answer.

Earning requires working, which calls for some self-discipline, and that brings in the big question of motivation. History is witness to the interesting relationship between strength and weakness of motivation and the rise and fall of civilizations, Islamic civilization being no exception. The Prophet (peace be upon him) had some strongly motivated people around him. Motivation is multi-dimensional, but here I am largely thinking of money making. Few remember that as many as four out of the ten Companions of the Prophet who were congratulated as they were promised a place in Jannah died billionaires, in today's terms. There is ample evidence that they worked hard for that kind of wealth, especially as some of them, like Abdur-Rahman ibn Auf, had migrated to Madinah empty handed. To the possible query, why earn so much? The answer that Islamic history provides with reference to men like Abdur-Rahman ibn Auf and Uthman ibn Affan, the celebrated third Caliph, lies in the last of the above sequence: giving.

Unfortunately, the self-confidence that makes a conscientious Muslim a big moneymaker in a life by definition transient and desired to be lived in preparation for the eternal life in the Hereafter was soon lost under the influence of Christian asceticism and, possibly, Greek and Hindu philosophies. A shadow was cast upon "earning." This raised alarm bells among the wise and the farsighted, inviting a spate of works titled The Book of Earning, beginning with *Kitab al-Kasb* by Imam Muhammad bin al-Hasan al-Shaybani (D.189 H/834 C.E.). These books, numbering a dozen over the next hundred years, argued in the light of texts from the Qur'an and Sunnah that it was permissible for a Muslim to earn, save, and invest. The first generation of Muslims had a vision of living that precluded the need for such arguments. Going further into this probe will, however, take us far from the limited scope of a fore-word, to a book making a plea for Muslims to take their finances seri-ously. Suffice it to say that something bigger than one's pleasure and the felicity of one's progeny is at stake.

Convince Muslims that they need not be very keen to earn and you have knocked the bottom out of the whole edifice; pulling down this one pillar threatens the whole structure with collapse. Sounds strange in twenty-first century America, where everybody is going crazy after earning. Well, have a second look at the recipe: earn, save, invest, spend, and give. Many Americans spend before they earn. Do not do that, the author says, as our beloved Prophet was averse to indebtedness, so much so that his supplications to God included seeking protection from being in debt. Reported supplications associate heavy indebtedness with bondage (*ghalabat al-dayn*).

Some venture to give without having saved and invested. Not sus-tainable, warns our money manager. You have to plan for giving in an efficient way. The idea of efficient giving should be pursued further; indeed organized philanthropy deserves a chapter in all textbooks on Islamic economics. Zakah, waqf, and charitable giving in general provide an important complement to market economy in Islam. The focus in the book is on how to calculate zakah-liability. The next step is how to organize zakah expenditure at community level so that its place in a fully functioning Islamic economy may be defined, where the state too plays a significant role besides the market and the voluntary sector, based on giving.

The "five pillars" of prosperity indicated by the author need not be envisioned as a straight path. Instead, they form a ring as the one on your finger. Earning-saving-investing enables you to spend and also creates an obligation to give; the urge to give prods good people to earn more, save, and invest. In between comes spending, which gives you comfort while boosting growth. It is a virtuous circle. Be serious about the entire circuit, if you want the current to flow and electrify your life.

The young Islamic community in North America will greatly benefit from the wealth-building strategies suggested by the author. It is a timely contribution. The community is passing through trying times when money would serve it well. I know of no other person better equipped than Dr. Yaqub Mirza to perform the *fard al-kifayah* of telling Muslims how to manage their finances.

Mohammad Nejatullah Siddiqi
Professor Emeritus
Faculty of Business Administration, Aligarh Muslim University

AUTHOR'S PREFACE

WHILE helping my father in our family business (I was 12 years old), I studied books of the Hadith (sayings of the Prophet Muhammad), which my father had in his library. Studying these books was a great learning experience in every respect. We discussed work ethics, the virtues of hard work, being persistent to achieve results, helping the needy, and supporting social services that are in keeping with one's faith.

During discussions around the concept of debt, my father used to remind me that God will forgive through His mercy everything except debt and wrongs done to others. These, he said, could be forgiven only by the aggrieved party, and on the Day of Judgment if they do not forgive you, then God will take your good deeds to recompense them.

This left a great impression on me. Growing up, I became very conscious of debt and wanted to avoid borrowing money and hurting someone's feelings. I vividly recall times when I was making a purchase and I had only part of the money; the shopkeepers (they knew me, as we were living in a small town) would say take the merchandise and pay the rest later. I would decline, telling them to hold the merchandise until I had the money to pay first; the thought being that if I took the item – while owing money and I died (on my way home) – my family wouldn't know I owed this money. "This will be a debt which I will have to deal with in the Hereafter."

This became a guiding principle in my life that pushed me to find ways for my family to pay for a car, a house, Hajj, my children's education, etc., without incurring debt (and paying interest). This led me to the study and practice (and ultimately putting this guide together) of the five key elements of money:

1st Pillar	2nd Pillar	3rd Pillar	4th Pillar	5th Pillar
Earning	*Saving*	*Investing*	*Spending*	*Giving*

This approach requires a lot of discipline, patience, and fortitude, and if you put in the effort to incorporate these in your life, you will soon achieve wealth and peace of mind, without financial worry.

Hopefully, by following this approach, you will soon have enough money to enjoy life and help others. Enjoy.

M. Yaqub Mirza,
Washington, D.C.

INTRODUCTION

IN today's climate of economic distress and uncertainty, people the world over have seen their assets and savings greatly diminished. Yet, as the Qur'an points out, with crisis comes opportunity: "Surely, with every difficulty there is relief" (Q 94:5–6). The recession has caused many to adopt a "back to basics" approach to finances. As individuals, families, and businesses struggle to regain the prosperity they once enjoyed, it has become more important than ever for them to master and control their finances. Many are now reconsidering the use of credit cards and borrowing even to cover essential life expenses. People are seeking ways of managing money that ensure consistent financial security while avoiding risky ventures and heavy borrowing of any kind.

THIS GUIDE PRESENTS THE ISLAMIC APPROACH TO FINANCE, WHICH IS BASED ON COMMONSENSE PRINCIPLES.

This guide presents the Islamic approach to finance, which is based on commonsense principles. As the Muslim scholar Irfan Ul Haq notes, Islam promotes the work ethic and private economic enterprise and urges the creation of wealth. Islam favors accumulation of wealth through saving and investment, and recycling of wealth through reinvestment on a continuous basis. It simultaneously discourages conspicuous consumption and suggests modest living. Islam argues that society should operate responsibly, work hard, and produce a caring and prosperous community. Taking care of its poor and needy and behaving ethically are at the heart of Islamic values! The Holy Qur'an encourages believers to engage in beneficial trade and to invest. In it, God encourages Muslims "not to eat up your [wealth] among yourselves in vanities: but let there be trade amongst you by mutual goodwill" (Q 4:29).

ISLAM, PERHAPS MORE THAN ANY OTHER MAJOR RELIGION OF THE WORLD, SEES FINANCE AS INTEGRAL WITH FAITH.

Financing that follows Islamic principles is relatively risk-averse. It focuses on building wealth for the long term in a way that does not put money in the pockets of creditors or in the hands of companies that are unethically directed. Islamic financial principles also prohibit purchasing or investing in any industry or company associated with vices such as alcohol, tobacco, gambling, and pornography, and they prohibit charging interest on loans.

Islam, perhaps more than any other major religion of the world, sees finance as integral with faith. For centuries, Muslims all over the world have directed business enterprises; financed ambitious and innovative projects; traded across deserts, oceans, and continents; and provided for their families in ways consistent with Islamic principles.

Islamic financial principles are based on Shari'ah law. With the help of jurists (Muslim legal scholars) Muslims employ a sophisticated understanding of economics as well as unique ways of making transactions to further their financial goals.

A financial system following Islamic principles is known as Shariʿah compliant. To be compliant, a transaction must not contradict the scriptures, although a transaction does not have to be mentioned in the scriptures to be acceptable.

- Any law that supports what is good and moral is considered Islamic. As long as it follows the values of justice, preservation of equity, and fairness, then the transaction is valid.
- The transaction must also use proper currency and be without ambiguity.

The Qur'an says:

> "Seek with the [wealth] which God has bestowed on thee, the Home of the Hereafter, nor forget your portion in this World: but do thou good, as God has been good to thee, and seek not [occasions for] mischief in the land: For God loves not those who do mischief" (Q 28:77). "And ordain for us that which is good, in this life and in the hereafter, behold, unto Thee have we turned in repentance!" (Q 7:156); and "Eat of the good things that We have provided for you and be grateful to God, if it is Him you worship" (Q 2:172).

Muslims in North America and Europe can live according to Islamic financial principles, especially as existing financial institutions begin to offer appropriate programs and new institutions are created to specifically meet Muslim needs. They can earn their living, deposit their savings, finance their cars and homes, insure their assets, charge their purchases, and make investment choices for their future and the future of their children in accordance with Islamic teachings.[1]

The Shariʿah is clear on certain key financial principles, including avoiding debt; neither earning nor paying interest; and the ethical use of wealth for supporting first oneself and one's family, then the larger community. We will look at these one by one.

REFRAIN FROM BORROWING AND INCURRING DEBT

Islam prefers that a person not be in a dependent position, so Muslims are strongly discouraged from incurring debt. Certainly giving in charity or spending for social welfare is better than being a recipient. A debt-free Muslim who saves wisely can then have enough money for a car, a college education, marriage (one's own or one's child's), hajj (pilgrimage), and umrah (travel to Makkah outside the pilgrimage season).

Lynnette Khalfani-Cox in her book *Zero Debt* states:

> Debt is the longest-lasting economic curse, the most heinous financial plague, and the least recognized form of modern slavery afflicting Americans (and others around the world) this millennium.[2]

Borrowing cannot be taken lightly. Borrowing by individuals and businesses may be necessary and beneficial in some situations, although arbitrary overextension is not a healthy practice.[3] If you must, then borrow moderately, and strive to repay the debt as soon as possible and continue to maintain more assets than liabilities (i.e., positive net worth). Go too much into debt and you will find yourself discredited.

THE PROPHET ALSO SAID HE SOUGHT REFUGE IN ALLAH (GOD) "FROM UNBELIEF AND DEBT."

Prophet Muhammad disliked it when people were in debt because debt worries the mind at night and is humiliating by day. It is recorded in the hadith, the record of the sayings of Muhammad, that he always asked God's protection from "the burden of debt and from the anger of men."[4] The Prophet also said he sought refuge in Allah (God) "from unbelief and debt," and that he equated debt with unbelief. In his prayers, he frequently said, "O Allah, I seek refuge in Thee from sin and debt." He was asked, "Why do you so often seek the protection of Allah from debt?" He replied, "One who is in debt tells lies and breaks promises."[5]

The Prophet strongly urged those able to repay the debt they had incurred to do so quickly as possible. A hadith states, "If a man borrows from people with the intention of repaying them, Allah will help him to repay, while if he borrows without intending to repay them, Allah will bring him to ruin."[6]

At the same time, the Qur'an teaches us to have mercy on the debtor.[7] "If the debtor is in difficulty, grant him time till it is easy for him to repay, if you remit it by way of charity it would be for your own good if you only knew" (Q 2:280).

AVOID INTEREST

Another element of the Islamic principles regarding finances is its prohibition regarding interest. Both paying and receiving interest are prohibited in Islam.

- The word riba, translated as "interest" or "usury" by different authors literally means increase, addition, expansion, or growth. In the Shariʿah, riba technically refers to the "premium" that the borrower must pay to the lender, along with the principal amount, for postponing, deferring, or waiting for a payment of the loan.[8]
- Riba includes both simple and compound interest. It refers to any money made on money, in contrast to money made by working or trade or by investing through equity partnership on a profit-loss-sharing basis.
- Riba in a loan is considered unjust, especially when the lender and borrower enter into an agreement on unequal terms, or when the lender is guaranteed a profit regardless of whether the borrower gains or loses money on the transaction.[9]
- With an interest-bearing loan the borrower repays the lender more than he has borrowed and previously received from him. Thus riba is like unearned income, in biblical terms the lender "reaps where he did not sow."

The Qur'an teaches about riba:

> "Devour not usury [riba], doubled and re-doubled" (Q 3:130). "O you who believe, Fear Allah, and give up what remains of your demand for usury, if you are indeed believers. If you do it not, take notice of war from Allah and his Messenger. But if you turn back, you shall have your capital sums; Deal not unjustly and you shall not be dealt with unjustly" (Q 2:278–279). "...He [Allah] has explained to you in detail what is forbidden to you except under compulsion of necessity" (Q 6:119).

This prohibition against interest also rules out interest-bearing investments, including conventional money market or money market mutual funds, certificates of deposit, corporate bonds, and U.S. Treasury bonds or T-bills. Some scholars have permitted sovereign bonds (*sukuk*), especially in Muslim countries.

The Jewish law with respect to interest is more qualified, permitting interest on a loan to a stranger but not on a loan to another Jew.

It says:

> On loans to a foreigner you may charge interest, but on loans to another Israelite you may not charge interest (Deuteronomy 23:20).

And:

> If you lend money to any of My people who are the poor among you, you shall not deal with them as a creditor; you shall not exact interest from them (Exodus 22:25).

The New Testament, on the other hand, reflects the commercial practices of the Roman Empire because Rome ruled in that part of the world during the lifetime of Jesus. Thus the New Testament assumes the legitimacy of banking, credit, and interest:

Then you ought to have invested my money with the bankers, and on my return I would have received what was my own with interest (Matthew 25:27).

MEET THE NEEDS OF FAMILY

While Islam supports the accumulation of wealth, it is clear regarding the proper use of this wealth: first to take care of the needs of oneself and one's family. The family bond among people bound together by blood ties and/or marital relationship entails mutual expectations of rights and obligations that are prescribed by religion and enforced by law. Accordingly, family members share certain mutual commitments. These pertain to identity, provision, inheritance, counsel, affection for the young, security for the aged, and maximization of effort to ensure continuity of the family.

GIVE SUPPORT TO COMMUNITY

After the immediate family receives benefit from these resources, and when any extended family (for example, aunts and uncles, in-laws, cousins) who are in need have been helped, our assistance should then extend to the larger community.

For Muslims living in North America or Europe today, the larger community includes people of other faiths, particularly the other two Abrahamic faiths, Judaism and Christianity.

These three religions are naturally suited to coexist and even to mutually reinforce each other. As one author explains:

> Being originally one religion, the three Abrahamic faiths worship the same God, although the three religions may differ in how they conceptualize that one God. God made this very point in the Qur'an when He said that the Muslims and the People of the Book [ahl al-kitab; i.e., Jews and Christians] have the same deity:

"our God and your God is One; and it is to Him we bow [in
Islam]."[10]

Few non-Muslims are aware that Prophet Muhammad, the messenger of Islam, preached that Jesus and Moses were the pre-Islamic
bearers of God's revelation to mankind. Islam recognizes both the Torah
and the New Testament, and texts from these scriptures are cited in the
Qur'an. As Christians believe the New Testament was the completion
of the "Old Testament" of Judaism, so Muslims believe the Qur'an is the
final completion of these books, and Muhammad is the last Prophet and
Messenger of God.[11]

Judaism, Christianity, and Islam all believe in God.[12] Whilst Jews and
Muslims greatly stress a strict monotheism (the oneness and unity of
God), the Christian idea of the Divine Being is more complex, with God
being one in essence and three in person (the Trinity).

All three religions believe that this God, the origin and source of all
that exists, is just and also merciful. He has provided basic rules for our
guidance so that we may be good and righteous, and by His grace we
are given the strength to be righteous.

Judaism, Christianity, and Islam also share common rituals and
practices (such as regular prayer and charity). All three value pilgrimage and share many common holy places; promise that behavior will
receive its proper rewards and punishments in the future, on earth and
in an afterlife; and balance and integrate strands of mysticism, legalism,
and pious devotion. Love of God and love of one's neighbors are the two
great commandments in Judaism, Christianity, and Islam. The New
Testament says:

> Love the Lord your God with all your heart and with all your soul
> and with all your mind and with all your strength. Love your
> neighbor as yourself (Mark 12:30-31).

The essence of Islam is to serve Allah and do good to your fellow-
creatures. This expands on the theme of "Love God and love your
neighbor." It includes duties to animals as our fellow creatures and

emphasizes service in addition to sentiment. As the Qur'an says:

> Serve Allah, and join not any partners with Him; and do good—
> to parents, relatives, orphans, those in need, neighbors who are
> near, neighbors who are strangers, the companion by your side,
> the wayfarer (you meet), and what your right hands possess: For
> Allah loveth not the proud and boastful ones (Q 4:36).

Many hadith enjoin good treatment of neighbors in general, regardless of whether they are relatives or not – and whether they are of the same religion or not. For example, the Prophet said:[13] "Jibrīl [Gabriel] kept urging me to treat neighbors kindly, until I thought that he would make neighbors heirs."[14] The *Ṣaḥābah* (Companions) heard this teaching of the Prophet, and they hastened to put it into practice in their daily lives with their own neighbors, both Muslims and non-Muslims. ʿAbd Allāh ibn ʿAmr, the great *Ṣaḥābī* (Companion), remembered this hadith when he slaughtered one of his sheep, and he asked his servant, "Did you give any to our Jewish neighbor? Did you give any to our Jewish neighbor? For I heard the Messenger of Allah say..."—and he quoted this hadith:[15] "He does not believe in me who goes to bed full when his neighbor beside him is hungry and he knows about that."[16]

The Qur'an repeatedly calls for universal cooperation among all races, peoples, and tribes. Muslims must deal kindly and justly with all those who have different beliefs from theirs, as long as they are not at war against Muslims on account of their faith nor have driven them out of their homes (Q 60:7-9).

These comments about the commonalities among the three Abrahamic religions are about similarities of faith and ethics. Similarly, the interfaith movement, which may include not only Jews, Christians, and Muslims but also Sikhs, Hindus, Buddhists, and others, has generally been focused on sharing scripture.

However, the core commonality we all have is not in our understanding of what God is or is not, but in the fact that we all live together on earth.[17] My friend and religious scholar Joseph Montville has beautifully expressed this interfaith perspective as follows:

The community may also include those who profess no religion, but still reflect God's guidance in their lives—individuals whose number would greatly expand the community. In the end, it is God only who judges who is worthy of salvation regardless of professed faith or none.[18]

The larger community is built around our shared love of God and love of the planet. Service to nature is the bond that connects people of all faiths. The environmental movement offers Muslims, Christians, Jews, and other faith congregants the opportunity to connect in a spirit of service to our shared earth. There are several charitable organizations (like FAITH: Foundation for Appropriate Immediate Temporary Help, located in Herndon, Virginia) striving to foster understanding and acceptance among adherents of the Abrahamic and other faiths. One such organization is the Centre for Abrahamic Religions developed through a collaborative effort among Durham University and Cambridge University in the U.K. and the University of Virginia in the U.S. The center, through its Scriptural Reasoning program, seeks to acknowledge and discover the commonalities and distinctiveness of the Tanakh, the Qur'an, and the Bible.

THE LARGER COMMUNITY IS BUILT AROUND OUR SHARED LOVE OF THE PLANET. SERVICE TO NATURE IS THE BOND THAT CONNECTS PEOPLE OF ALL FAITHS.

While I am not trained in nor do I profess to interpret the scripture, I do envision a world in which we the people find the ways and means to "commune." I accept the fact that others have no wish to convert to Islam but are willing to learn from one another and live in peace and harmony. It may not be easy, but I believe this is the only way we can all progress and coexist as human beings on this planet Earth. To live in a compassionate "global community" we must treat others like we ourselves wish to be treated.

HOW THE PROPHET MUHAMMAD IMPLEMENTED THE CONCEPT OF PLURALISM

The Prophet established the first pluralistic, multi-faith state. The state of Yathrib, which was founded by the Messenger, was formed of various groups of people, who are mentioned in the text of the *Saheefah*, a kind of "Constitution," which was drawn up by the Prophet. This was similar in many ways to the modern political concept of the state, which is defined by the groups living in the state and the land where they live. The Prophet did not restrict his community to only one group that followed one particular religion. He included in it the Muslims who had migrated from Makkah (the *muhajirun*), the Muslim inhabitants of Madinah (the *ansar*), and the Jews who were with them. He said concerning all of these people in the *Saheefah*: "They are one nation, distinct from other people." This concept is now known as pluralism or described as a multi-cultural community.

Allah willed that this new Islamic state should be recorded for the first time in history in a constitutional document that was approved of by all parties.

Lay congregations can come together and work together. This work will consist of radically altering our way of thinking about development, profit, gain, and loss. We need to connect with those of other faiths to raise our children as part of a larger community of "people of faith." We make these connections through establishing community gardens, engaging in cleanup efforts, renovating or replacing old buildings, and salvaging useful materials.

One such example is the Masjid At-Taqwa in Brooklyn, New York. When Imam Siraj Wahhaj and his colleagues purchased the building at 1266 Bedford Avenue in Brooklyn back in the early 1980s, it was an abandoned clothing store. Their first job was to expel the drug users and dealers. Thanks to joint efforts between the police and Muslims organized by Imam Wahhaj, the area was successfully reclaimed from drugs and crime. Today, the "mosque of God-consciousness" serves as a symbol of the neighborhood's flourishing "Muslim economy," which includes a deli, a convenience store, and a Halal restaurant. "Those who have faith and do righteous deeds – they are the best of creatures" (Q 98:7).

TODAY'S NEED FOR THE FIVE PILLARS OF PROSPERITY

The global community of today is both fortunate and challenged. We are experiencing a proliferation of opportunities available to more people than ever before in history. At the same time, we live in a world that is obsessed with money: acquiring it, possessing it, and spending it (and sometimes showing off too!). **The purpose of money is to serve as a medium of exchange for goods and services.** In today's world, however, it has come to represent power and prestige. This is a rattrap – one that can be quite destructive.

THERE IS A WAY OUT

The way out is to understand and then build your financial life upon the five pillars of prosperity: to become masters of earning, saving, investing, spending, and giving. This guide can be used as a starting point, and the time to start the process is today. In the following chapters we will discuss each of these elements in detail, and this five-step financial program can be summarized as follows:

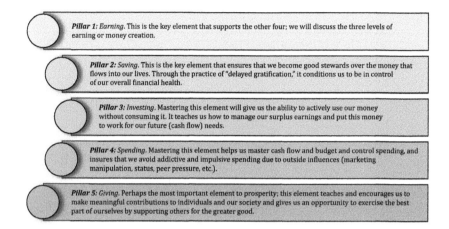

Pillar 1: *Earning.* This is the key element that supports the other four; we will discuss the three levels of earning or money creation.

Pillar 2: *Saving.* This is the key element that ensures that we become good stewards over the money that flows into our lives. Through the practice of "delayed gratification," it conditions us to be in control of our overall financial health.

Pillar 3: *Investing.* Mastering this element will give us the ability to actively use our money without consuming it. It teaches us how to manage our surplus earnings and put this money to work for our future (cash flow) needs.

Pillar 4: *Spending.* Mastering this element helps us master cash flow and budget and control spending, and insures that we avoid addictive and impulsive spending due to outside influences (marketing manipulation, status, peer pressure, etc.).

Pillar 5: *Giving.* Perhaps the most important element to prosperity; this element teaches and encourages us to make meaningful contributions to individuals and our society and gives us an opportunity to exercise the best part of ourselves by supporting others for the greater good.

According to Islamic financial principles, a person's first financial duty is to take care of the needs of self and family – to earn the money, to save it by keeping daily expenditures less than income, and to invest the money so it will increase. In addition to daily expenditures, one can plan in order to spend intelligently on big-ticket expenditures of a constructive nature, such as education and hajj.

Finally, after the daily and big-ticket needs of family are met, one can give in order to help the larger community, as formalized in the Islamic practices of zakah and sadaqa, as well as other forms of giving while living. In this guide, you will find practical tools for managing money and building wealth. The approach in this book is faith-based, but one does not need to be Muslim to utilize this book and benefit from it.

EARNING

❝ FAR AND AWAY THE BEST PRIZE THAT LIFE HAS TO OFFER IS THE CHANCE TO WORK HARD AT WORK WORTH DOING. ❞
Theodore Roosevelt

IN the twenty-first century, earning – the ability to generate income – is more complex and fluid than at any other time in history. While the principles surrounding investing and business ownership have largely remained constant, employment and what it means to be employed are undergoing significant changes. Within these changes lie earning opportunities for those who have the eyes to see them and the courage to act on them.

Earning, the first pillar of prosperity, makes prosperity possible; it is the foundation upon which the other four pillars are built. Earning is thus fundamental to our livelihood.

❝ ACCUMULATION OF WEALTH IS NOT EVIL OF ITSELF, RATHER IT IS INTENTION TO USE WEALTH FOR PERSONAL AGGRANDIZEMENT THAT CONSTITUTE THE PROBLEM. ACCUMULATION FOR PIOUS PURPOSES SUCH AS PROVIDING FOR ONESELF AND ONE'S FAMILY, AND SHARING WITH OTHERS, IS QUITE LEGITIMATE. ❞
Ibn al-Jawzī (1292-1328)

MEANS OF LIVELIHOOD AND SUSTENANCE ON EARTH

The Qur'an points to the matter of livelihood as inseparable from being alive as a human being.[19] It states: "On earth will be your dwelling place and your means of livelihood for a time" (Q 2:36; see also 7:24). This verse addresses Adam and Eve, but it is applicable to all humankind for all times.

The Qur'an further says that our means of livelihood is given by God: "It is We who have placed you [humankind] with authority [or ability] on earth, and provided you therein with means for the fulfillment of your life [*maᶜāyish*]: small are the thanks you give" (Q 7:10). Similarly, "And We have provided therein means of subsistence for you [humankind] and for those for whose sustenance you are not responsible" (Q 15:20).

We acquire our livelihood through work. One of the Qur'anic principles is that "man can have nothing but what he strives for" (Q 53:39). This has a spiritual meaning and it also has a worldly meaning: earnings come through work, and when a person works they will see the fruit of that effort, which will be fully rewarded in Heaven (Q 53:39–41).

EARNING MONEY

In today's society, money is essential for living. Livelihoods are earned and wealth is accumulated and shared in the form of money. Because of money's importance, many people regard it as a form of protection from harm and hardship, which encourages a "survival-based" attitude around money. But basing one's survival on something – in this case, money – that is outside oneself causes apprehension or fear. This is the reason for the anxiety around money that is rampant in society today.

In fact, money is simply a medium of exchange. What fundamentally keeps us alive is our faith, vitality, and strength of spirit – not money. Money is a medium of exchange in return for value given. Our ability to generate money is directly linked to our ability to generate value in the

lives of others. This value may be given to a person, a company, a project, or an enterprise.

In general, the more the world values what you generate, the more money will be given to you. However, not all value is equal. There are essentially three factors that determine your ability to generate money through providing value:

THERE ARE ESSENTIALLY THREE FACTORS THAT DETERMINE YOUR ABILITY TO GENERATE MONEY THROUGH PROVIDING VALUE:
• THE UNIQUENESS (OR POSSIBLY EXCLUSIVITY) OF WHAT YOU ARE OFFERING.
• THE "FOOTPRINT" OF WHAT YOU OFFER, THAT IS, THE NUMBER OF PEOPLE WHO BENEFIT FROM IT

•THE IMPACT YOUR OFFERING HAS ON SOMEONE ELSE.

- The uniqueness (or possibly exclusivity) of what you are offering.
- The "footprint" of what you offer, that is, the number of people who benefit from it.
- The impact your offering has on someone else.

The degree of value you offer with regard to each of these three factors determines the amount of money you receive in exchange.

What kinds of activities are involved in earning money? Basically, there are three types: you make money for yourself, other people make money for you, and your investments make money for you. I will discuss these one by one.

You make money for yourself. The majority of the world's population earns money by making it for themselves. People working in every job classification – whether they be doctors, engineers, pilots, gardeners, grocery clerks, or factory workers – trade their time for money. The challenge with this method of earning is that a person's time is finite – and thus so is the person's income. Hence, if you become unable to trade your time for money, you've lost your source of income.

Other people make money for you. For small-business owners and other individuals involved in entrepreneurial pursuits, revenue and ultimately profit are generated by the activities of the business and the efforts of its employees. This makes better use of the business owner's time, since the time of several people is focused on earning money for the business and, ultimately, for the owner. It is also more stable, since if one person cannot work, others are present to take up the slack. Small-business owners and other individuals involved in entrepreneurial pursuits fall in this category.

Your investments make money for you. Earning a profit on investments is the optimal earning strategy, although only a small percentage of the world's population effectively uses it. Using money to make money requires knowledge and skill – and money. Sadly, most people, whether due to lack of knowledge, living paycheck to paycheck, or for other reasons, are unable to earn money through investments. That said, many people can eventually earn money this way if they follow the five principles outlined in this book. Here again, the key ingredient, besides money, is time, since the length of time the money is invested factors significantly in the success or failure of most investments.

EMPLOYMENT

The great majority of us start out our professional journey employed. But I would advise the following: **While working as an employee, start seeing things with the eyes of an owner.**

- Whether your employer is a big or small company, take the opportunity to experience and grow as much as possible. Learn to become aware of what impact your work has on the organization's success, and you will start to develop an appreciation for things beyond your job.

My advice to younger readers aspiring to have a successful career, who may be contemplating eschewing more traditional professions for the latest and greatest, such as high technology and other highly visible and apparently lucrative endeavors, is this: **be diligent in your research of any career track you are considering.**

MY PERSONAL MOTTO HAS BEEN "IF SOMEONE ELSE CAN DO MY JOB, THEN I AM NOT DOING MY JOB." WE MUST PERSIST AND EXCEL AT WHAT WE DO AND, HOPEFULLY, DO IT BETTER THAN OTHERS.

- You may want to read Richard N. Bolles' *What Color Is Your Parachute?* book series. It provides a practical and systematic approach to discovering career and job choices that would be most appropriate for you. Such books are extremely helpful to anyone wishing to change jobs or career tracks as well.

My personal motto has been "If someone else can do my job, then I am not doing my job." We must persist and excel at what we do and, hopefully, do it better than others.

ENTREPRENEURSHIP

With the development of information technology and the growth of the internet as a marketplace, it is becoming easier for more people to become entrepreneurs. As this entrepreneurial trend grows, it is essential that people of faith take leadership roles as entrepreneurs. The world needs business owners who can ensure the call of God as they help build and lead society through faith-based businesses.[20]

Becoming an Entrepreneur

The combination of faith and entrepreneurship has been modeled in Islam from its very beginning.

Prophet Muhammad himself was an influential and successful businessman and a trader. He was known for always charging fair prices and never hoarding any goods. Because of this, the people of Makkah dubbed him *al-Ṣādiq* and *al-Amīn* (the Truthful and the Trustworthy).

Getting over fear

Trust your instincts - imagine the worst - and just do it

Pillar Two

SAVING

THE Islamic economic doctrine emphasizes hard work, productivity, and the generation of surplus. The surplus makes possible saving, whether for future contingencies, posterity, or other purposes – such as investing, making major purchases, or giving to help the needy and supporting projects of public good. Therefore, while the first pillar of prosperity is to generate sufficient income to meet the current consumption needs of the individual and their family, the second pillar is to generate savings.

THE CORNERSTONE OF ACHIEVING FINANCIAL FREEDOM IS THE RECOGNITION THAT YOU ARE RESPONSIBLE FOR YOUR OWN FINANCIAL WELL-BEING, AND THE DESIRE TO SAVE IS THE FIRST STEP TO FINANCIAL FREEDOM.

Some people think spirituality and saving do not go together. But there is nothing unspiritual about having money set aside for investments and for future needs. This does not in any way show a lack of trust in God's provisions. Prophet Muhammad used to urge his Companions to be prudent by not spending all that they had. The Qur'an recounts how, in times of plenty, Prophet Yūsuf (Joseph) organized great reserves to meet the needs of famine (Q 12:47–49). Author Dwight Nichols, a Christian, points out in *God's Plans for Your Finances* that, according to the scriptures (Proverbs 6:6–8 and 21:20), a person who stores in times of plenty and prepares for winter is wise.

"O YOU WHO BELIEVE! YOU HAVE CHARGE OVER YOUR OWN SOULS."

The cornerstone of achieving financial freedom is the recognition that you are responsible for your own financial well-being, and the desire to save is the first step to financial freedom. The Qur'an also wants you to be cognizant of your own financial activities and their effects on yourself, your family, and others: "O you who believe! You have charge over your own souls" (Q 5:105). Unfortunately, too few people in America today are following this commonsense wisdom. Here are a few sobering statistics generated by Scottrade's 2011 American Retirement Survey:

- Almost half (47 percent) of Baby Boomers (Americans born between 1945 and 1966) have $100,000 or less saved, and more than a third (37 percent) are concerned that they will have to work in their retirement years.
- Almost a quarter (23 percent) think they'll still be working at age 75 or older.
- A majority of Baby Boomers (58 percent) say that, if given a second chance, they would have started saving at a younger age.
- The majority (55 percent) of Gen Yers (Americans born between

1983 and 1992) have not started to save for retirement.

Warren Buffet gives the following advice:[21]

- Live your life as simply as you can.
- Don't be seduced by the brand label; instead wear things that are made well and are comfortable.
- Avoid wasteful spending.
- Manage your life and priorities so that you can live on less than you earn, saving 20% (or preferably 30% or more) on all that you make.

Is a penny saved a penny earned, as Benjamin Franklin said? Not quite, because a penny saved is really equal to one and a half pennies earned; that is, it is the amount you would have after paying taxes on 1.5 pennies. How is this so? Federal, state, and sales taxes combined are approximately 33 percent. Therefore, $1.50 earned – .50 tax (33% of $1.50) = $1.00 net. So when you spend $1.00, pause and think, because you are really spending $1.50 earned. Conversely, if you cut expenses and save $1.00, you are really earning $1.50.

❝ IF YOU MAKE A GOOD INCOME EACH YEAR AND SPEND IT ALL, YOU ARE NOT GETTING WEALTHIER. YOU ARE JUST LIVING HIGH. ❞
Thomas J. Stanley and William D. Danko, The Millionaire Next Door

A FEW THOUGHTS ON MOVING TOWARDS DEBT-FREE LIVING

During the research for the book, I've run across many sources offering suggestions on moving towards a debt-free life. Most of these suggestions fall in one of two camps. In one, most take what I would consider a technical approach to debt elimination – establishing (and living to) a budget, negotiations with creditors (to reduce or eliminate debt), and concepts like "debt acceleration." The other camp takes a more creative approach: coupon clipping, timing of purchases to exploit

sales, bulk purchase schemes and other means of "stretching" the dollar.
Both camps can lead you to the same road – a road of debt-free living. And for those of you who may find these strategies too extreme, what follows is a blend from both camps that I believe could serve you well.

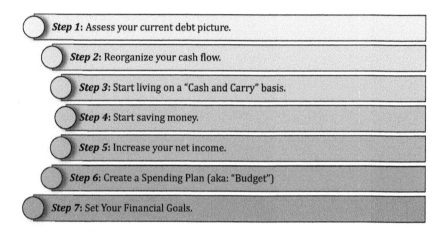

Step 1: Assess your current debt picture.

Step 2: Reorganize your cash flow.

Step 3: Start living on a "Cash and Carry" basis.

Step 4: Start saving money.

Step 5: Increase your net income.

Step 6: Create a Spending Plan (aka: "Budget")

Step 7: Set Your Financial Goals.

Small expenses definitely add up, especially when we treat "wants" as "necessities." Starbucks's 2011 revenue was $11.7 billion (the equivalent of $37.36 for every American) – a clear indication of how much Americans are spending for "wants."[22]

SMALL EXPENSES DEFINITELY ADD UP, ESPECIALLY WHEN WE TREAT "WANTS" AS "NECESSITIES."

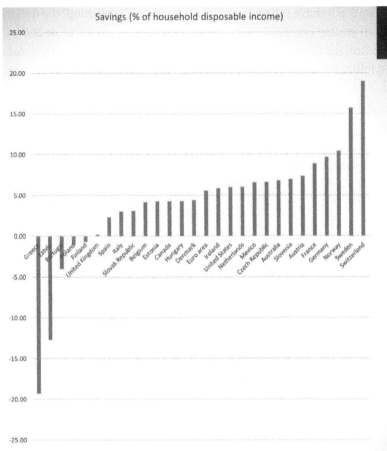

Household Savings Rate (% of household disposable income)

Source: OECD: National Accounts at a Glance

INVESTING

❝ INVESTING FOR PROFIT IS NOT EASY. ❞
M. Yaqub Mirza

MANY people make the mistake of looking at investing as a means to becoming wealthy. In fact, true wealth cannot be "purchased"; it is, instead, a state of mind. Your wealth consists of not only material things but also less tangible things such as your health, your time, your relationships (with family, loved ones, and the community), your generosity, and your heart. The sole purpose of investing is to generate income.

THE FIRST RULE OF MAKING MONEY IS TO NOT LOSE IT: IF YOU DO NOT UNDERSTAND THE INVESTMENT, DO NOT INVEST IN IT.

Investing, besides increasing one's own wealth, has social value. Irfan Ul Haq comments on the benefits of both private and social investments. When savings are invested as private investments (through nonpublic markets), they create goods and jobs, generate income, improve the living standard, and bring monetary reward to the investor.

For this reason, private investing is meritorious and rewardable in the eyes of God.

Similarly, when savings are invested as social investments (for the betterment of society), they benefit the recipients, meeting their immediate needs and raising their living standard while also adding to aggregate demand and creating jobs and income through the multiplier effect. Social investing is therefore rewarded several-fold while allowing the purification and "sweetening" (*tazkiyah*) of the investor's wealth.[23]

I learned the value of investing early on through personal experience. In the early 1970's, when I was a graduate student, I saved about $200 a month (65 percent of my income). When I became a postdoctoral fellow, this amount increased to about $500 a month. By 1980, I had accumulated around $53,000.

These funds, which were invested at a 10 percent rate of return on average, grew to $120,000 by the time my wife and I built our house, and to $266,000 by the time our oldest child was ready to go to college. By continuing to add some portion of our savings to these funds over time, we had enough to cover college-related expenses for our three other children and part of the purchase price of our house and cars.

WHAT MAKES INVESTING OVER A LONG PERIOD OF TIME LIKE THIS SO SUCCESSFUL IS THE POWER OF COMPOUNDING.

Time plays two key roles in wealth-building activities. It is the determining factor in the effectiveness of compounding income. And it is an ally with regard to your investment "time horizon," meaning that the more time you have to invest, the more likely it is that good years will offset bad years and your investment's return will come close to the long-term average that you expect.

THE BEST WAY TO BUILD A SIZEABLE ESTATE IS TO START EARLY. THE NEXT BEST WAY IS TO START AT ONCE.

As a businessman, investor, and active member of the Muslim community, I am often approached by people seeking investment advice. What follows are several key pieces of advice I can offer about investing:

Table 3.1: *Comparison of Total Accumulation of Funds by Age 65*

AGE	Sana Investing began at age 14 (10% Annual Return)		Maryam Investing began at age 19 (10% Annual Return)		Julie Investing began at age 27 (10% Annual Return)	
	INVEST.	TOTAL	INVEST.	TOTAL	INVEST.	TOTAL
14	$2,000	$2,200				
15	2,000	4,620				
16	2,000	7,282				
17	2,000	10,210				
18	2,000	13,431				
19	0	14,774	$2,000	$2,200		
20	0	16,252	2,000	4,600		
21	0	17,877	2,000	7,282		
22	0	19,665	2,000	10,210		
23	0	21,631	2,000	13,431		
24	0	23,794	2,000	16,974		
25	0	26,174	2,000	20,871		
26	0	28,791	2,000	25,158		
27	0	31,670	0	27,674	$2,000	$2,200
28	0	34,837	0	30,442	2,000	4,620
29	0	38,321	0	33,486	2,000	7,282
30	0	42,153	0	36,834	2,000	10,210
31	0	46,368	0	40,518	2,000	13,431
32	0	51,005	0	44,570	2,000	16,974
33	0	56,106	0	48,027	2,000	20,871
34	0	61,716	0	53,929	2,000	25,158

Table 3.1: *Continued*

AGE	Sana INVEST.	Sana TOTAL	Maryam INVEST.	Maryam TOTAL	Julie INVEST.	Julie TOTAL
35	0	67,888	0	59,322	2,000	29,874
36	0	74,676	0	65,256	2,000	35,072
37	0	82,144	0	71,780	2,000	40,768
38	0	90,359	0	78,958	2,000	47,045
39	0	99,394	0	86,854	2,000	53,949
40	0	109,334	0	95,540	2,000	61,544
41	0	120,267	0	105,094	2,000	69,899
42	0	132,294	0	115,603	2,000	79,089
43	0	145,523	0	127,163	2,000	89,198
44	0	160,076	0	139,880	2,000	100,318
45	0	176,083	0	153,868	2,000	112,550
46	0	193,692	0	169,255	2,000	126,005
47	0	213,061	0	188,180	2,000	140,805
48	0	234,367	0	204,798	2,000	157,086
49	0	257,803	0	226,278	2,000	174,094
50	0	283,358	0	247,806	2,000	194,694
51	0	311,942	0	272,586	2,000	216,363
52	0	343,136	0	299,845	2,000	240,199
53	0	377,450	0	329,830	2,000	266,419
54	0	415,195	0	362,813	2,000	295,261
55	0	456,715	0	399,094	2,000	326,988
56	0	502,386	0	439,003	2,000	361,886
57	0	552,625	0	482,904	2,000	400,275
58	0	607,887	0	531,194	2,000	442,503
59	0	668,676	0	584,314	2,000	488,953
60	0	735,543	0	642,745	2,000	540,048
61	0	809,098	0	707,020	2,000	596,253
62	0	890,007	0	777,722	2,000	658,078
63	0	979,008	0	855,494	2,000	726,086
64	0	1,076,909	0	941,043	2,000	800,895
65	0	1,184,600	0	1,035,148	2,000	883,185

Total invested = $10,000	Total invested = $16,000	Total invested = $78,000
Earning beyond investment = $1,174,600	Earning beyond investment = $1,019,148	Earning beyond investment = $805,185

SET UP AN INVESTMENT STRATEGY

The first key piece of investing advice is to have a strategy. When it comes to investments, many people are simply confused. As often as not, their investments are nothing more than a haphazard collection that accumulated over time without careful planning, though each investment may have seemed good at the time of purchase. The results of a lack of planning can be risky, leaving people short of achieving important financial goals, such as having sufficient retirement income or money for their children's college education.

SELECTING AN INVESTMENT STRATEGY MAY SEEM LIKE A DIFFICULT TASK. IN FACT, IT IS NOT SO DIFFICULT. FOCUSING ON YOUR LONG-TERM FINANCIAL GOALS (WHERE YOU WANT TO BE IN SEVERAL YEARS) IS THE STARTING POINT.

Step 1: Take Your Financial Inventory
Pull out your financial records on stock investments, mutual funds, or other liquid assets. Add the value of your house or condominium. Search for hidden assets like retirement plans, IRAs (individual retirement accounts), life insurance policies, and so forth. Once you have located your assets, total them up. Then subtract any debts you have: mortgages on real estate, taxes you owe but have not yet paid, credit card balances, home equity loans. The resulting figure is your net worth.

Step 2: Create Your Emergency Fund
Once you have completed your inventory, set aside an emergency fund,

which should be about six months' expenses. You should not take even modest investment risks until you have accumulated enough funds to cover your basic emergency needs.

Step 3: Determine Your Risk Tolerance

Next, determine the amount of investment risk you can afford to take. Generally, the longer it will be until you need your money, the greater the risk you can afford because you have the time to ride out temporary drops in the value of your investments.

On the other hand, if you will need your money soon – perhaps you are nearing retirement and will need the money to pay expenses – you should limit your investment risks. You do not want to take the chance of having to raise funds for living expenses at a time when the value of your portfolio is temporarily low.

Furthermore, if you are the sort of person who can't sleep at night because your portfolio is temporarily down even a little in value, then you should definitely limit the risk you take. Peace of mind is important.

Step 4: Create an Investment Portfolio

The next step is to construct a diversified portfolio that blends many types of investments in order to lessen the risk associated with limiting yourself to only a particular investment. A diversified portfolio might include several types of investments: stocks, profit-sharing funds, real estate, and precious metals. For the Muslim investor who desires to follow Shariʿah, many kinds of investments present a problem because the type of business type is unacceptable or the company pays interest. For this reason, stocks play an unusually important role for Muslim investors.

ANOTHER KEY PIECE OF ADVICE FOR SUCCESSFUL INVESTING IS TO CONSULT AN INVESTMENT PROFESSIONAL.

Of course, the Muslim investor must pay attention to the companies in which they hold stock to be sure they follow practices con-sistent with Islamic principles. This isn't always easy. Coca-Cola, for example, may appear to be simply a soft drink company, but it also has large holdings in the wine business, which is prohibited for investment by Muslims.

Step 5: Consult an Investment Professional
Another key piece of advice for successful investing is to consult an investment professional. In fact, not working with a professional is often the primary reason people do not reap the full potential of their investments.

Above all, do not buy something just because an "expert," such as the ones you see on CNBC, recommended buying it. Consider this: How will you know when that same expert will sell it?

Step 6: Educate Yourself
Successful investing requires some effort to educate yourself. The best investors spend time learning about the markets they are investing in.

I can recommend several great books to help you get started. Burton Malkiel's *A Random Walk Down Wall Street* is a timeless classic, and Warren Buffett's Berkshire *Hathaway Letters to Shareholders: 1965–2012* reveals his views on business and investing. Peter Lynch's *Learn to Earn* is an excellent primer for young investors, while *The Intelligent Investor*, by Benjamin Graham, is an advanced book that may prove valuable once you have gained some experience with the markets.

Step 7: Take a Consistent Approach
Another key to successful long-term investing is consistency. Most individual investors tend to be market followers, investing when things seem to be going well and selling (or at least holding off on investing) when things don't look so good. However, following the market violates the basic rule of investing: buy low and sell high. For the majority of investors, a consistent and disciplined approach is important.

SELECT YOUR STRATEGY, STICK TO IT

PICK YOUR INVESTMENTS, ACCORDINGLY,

AND MAKE YOUR INVESTMENTS
CONSISTENTLY.

Step 8: Seek Out Faith-Based Investments

In addition to developing an investment strategy, consulting a professional, and being consistent with their investing strategy, investors who
wish to follow the principles of Islam have special needs to be met.
Following Islamic financial principles, Muslims tend to avoid speculation, in the sense of uninformed, undisciplined betting on the future.
Many Muslims avoid futures contracts or investments that are not
backed by a tangible asset or identifiable service. And Muslim investors
want to their investments to be Shariʿah compliant.

Faith-Based Mutual Funds

Because mutual funds offer a selected portfolio of investments, they can
be designed to follow certain chosen guidelines, including those dic-
tated by principles of faith.

Today there are several mutual funds designed to meet Islamic
requirements, such as Amana Income Fund (AMANX), Amana Growth
Fund (AMAGX), Imam Fund (IMANX), Azzad Ethical Mid Cap Fund
(ADJEX), Azzad – The Wise Capital (WISEX), and the Amana Developing
World Fund (AMDWX). These funds avoid interest (riba) by not
investing in bonds and other fixed-income securities. Nor do they invest
in businesses that deal in goods and services considered harmful by
Shariʿah law. These funds seek to offset inflation by making long-term
equity investments.

Investments following Islamic principles adhere to the following:

1. Transactions must be free of interest ("unearned income").
2. Money in itself should not be used to produce money. There
    should be direct participation in an economic activity.
3. Competition is encouraged, in contrast to monopoly. Eliminating
    monopoly is regarded as a prerequisite to justice and growth.

4.   Bribery and stealing are prohibited.
5.   Justice and fairness in all aspects of business transaction are required.
6.   Transactions must be documented and witnessed.
7.   Each person must be given their due share.
8.   Productive enterprise, cooperation, and development must be encouraged.
9.   Development efforts must include social development. Individual cooperation must be voluntary, not forced.
10.   Hoarding of money is strictly prohibited. One of the purposes of zakah is to discourage hoarding (and encourage investments).
11.   Unnecessary destruction of nature is prohibited, but moderate exploitation of resources is allowed.
12.   Labor should be valued and must be compensated. Laborers should get their fair remuneration without delay.
13.   Speculation is not allowed.
14.   Harmful goods and services cannot be produced, consumed, or traded. These are the following: alcohol, tobacco, pork-related products, unjust financial services (conventional banking, i.e., interest-based banks or savings and loan associations), weapons used to suppress people or for mass destruction, immoral entertainment (casinos, gambling, pornography, etc.), illegal drugs, harmful products (items that cause pain or suffering under normal use), transactions must be documented and witnessed.

Modes of Islamic Financing

One of the current trends in finance these days is the growing interest in socially responsible financing, a quest that Islam supports. Islamic finance promotes universal human improvement and, along the way, yields a fairer distribution of benefits than most conventional finance approaches. The following Islamic financial principles are being further developed and refined in various types of financial arrangements:

Muḍārabah (Profit Sharing). Muḍābarah is a contract under which the two parties, the supplier of capital and the entrepreneur (general partner), share the profits according to an agreed-upon profit-loss-sharing (PLS) ratio. The PLS ratio is typically 50:50 or 40:60.

- The first key element of a *muḍārabah* contract is that the financier or investor is not guaranteed a specific profit. There is no fixed annual or monthly payment. This is in direct contrast to conventional interest-based lending and financing, in which a loan is not contingent upon the profit or loss of the enterprise, requires monthly payments, and is normally secured by a collateral.

- The second key element is that the financier or investor is not liable for losses beyond the capital they have contributed, and the entrepreneur does not share in financial losses except for the loss of their time and effort.

Mushārakah (Joint Venture). *Mushārakah* is a partnership contract between two or more parties, each of which contributes investment capital.

- The first element of a *mushārakah* contract is that both parties contribute capital. Profits are shared by a prearranged agreement, not necessarily in proportion to their capital contribution. In case of loss, parties share in proportion to their capital contribution.

- The second element is that all parties share in determining how the investment is managed. Thus any partner has the right to examine the enterprise's books and supervise its management. The third element is that liability is unlimited.

Murābaḥah. *Murābaḥah* is a cost-plus-profit margin contract whereby the financier purchases an asset on behalf of the entrepreneur and sells it, usually at a profit or higher price, to the entrepreneur at a predetermined price, paid over time.

- The key characteristic of a *Murābaḥah*, a sales contract with the profit disclosed to the buyer, is the main tool of modern Islamic finance. The nature of *murābaḥah* is to sell and give credit by allowing deferred payment. Because *murābaḥah* discloses the seller's price and profit, and results in credit, many global banking authorities permit it as a credit instrument.

Ijārah (Leasing). In an *ijārah* contract, the financier purchases the asset on behalf of the entrepreneur and allows him or her to use it for a fixed rental payment. The entrepreneur may eventually opt to buy the assets at a previously agreed upon price.

- The key characteristic of *ijārah* is that ownership of the asset remains with the financier or is gradually transferred to the entrepreneur as the lease payments are made.

Istiṣnāʿ (Manufacturing Finance). *Istiṣnāʿ* is a contract of exchange with deferred delivery applied to specified made-to-order items. General principles of this practice are difficult to identify; however, very often the following are true:

- The nature and quality of the item to be delivered must be specified.
- The manufacturer must make a commitment to produce the item as described.
- The delivery date is not fixed; rather, the item is deliverable upon completion by the manufacturer.
- The contract is irrevocable after the commencement of manufacture except where delivered goods do not meet the contracted terms.
- Payment can be made in one lump sum or in installments, and at any time up to or after the time of delivery.
- The manufacturer is responsible for sourcing the inputs to the production process.

Istiṣnāʿ differs from *ijāra* (rent or lease) in that the manufacturer must procure the raw materials. Otherwise the contract would amount to hiring the seller's wage labor, as occurs under *ijāra*. *Istiṣnāʿ* also differs from *bayʿ al-salam* in that (a) the subject matter of the contract is always a made-to-order item, (b) the delivery date need not be fixed in advance, (c) full advance payment is not required, and (d) the *istiṣnāʿ* contract can be canceled but only before the seller commences manufacture of the item.

Qarḍ al-ḥasan (Benevolence Loan). Qarḍ al-ḥasan, a zero-return loan, or negative investment, is a great vehicle for community development. It is not a profit-making transaction; it is a social service vehicle providing an interest-free loan to an individual in need or to an organization.

Takāful (Pooled Money for Emergencies). Takāful is a type of Islamic insurance in which members contribute money into a pooling system in order to guarantee each other against loss or damage. It offers an alternative to conventional life, property, and car insurance. The principles of *takāful* are as follows:

- Policyholders cooperate among themselves for their common good.
- Every policyholder pays their subscription to help those who need assistance.
- Losses are divided and liabilities spread according to the community pooling system.
- Uncertainty is eliminated concerning subscription and compensation.
- No advantage is derived at the cost of others.

Pillar Four

SPENDING

SPENDING and saving are closely intertwined. For the purposes of this guide, I define spending as "planned spending, save, invest and then spend."

In a lifetime, you can save a tremendous amount of money by learning to spend wisely. Learning this skill is just as important as developing the habit of saving your hard-earned cash. In fact, it's more important, because there is no end to spending. When spending is not under control, it can negatively impact every area of your financial life.

ONE OF THE EASIEST WAYS TO SPEND YOUR MONEY IN A DELIBERATE AND CONSCIOUS MANNER IS TO ESTABLISH A PERSONAL BUDGET – A SPENDING PLAN.

Planning helps to condition your thinking and shape your behavior when it comes to spending money. It teaches you to become aware of the money going out for the items vital to living (such as groceries, rent, mortgage, car payment, debt repayment, utilities) and to manage your impulses to buy things you don't necessarily need. At the same time, it allows you to plan for purchasing things you want but may not need – things that improve the quality of life, like education, owning a car or a house, and hajj. How to spend intelligently on these and similar items is the topic of this chapter.

STEPS TO SPENDING MONEY WISELY

The following three steps will take you well down the road toward mastering spending:

The first step is to learn to control your impulses. Especially in the United States, we're conditioned at a very early age to consume, and to consume from impulse. By conducting most of your major spending from plans and budgets, you'll begin to limit impulsive purchases.

The second step is to give yourself time before making any major purchases. Sellers of big-ticket items have made it very easy for people to make a quick purchase. A car dealer can arrange a test drive, craft an offer, and get you into an executed contract on a new vehicle within a matter of hours. The intelligent approach is to take the time necessary to properly research and evaluate your options before setting foot into the dealership.

The third step is to get in the habit of using cash or a debit card for most purchases. This habit alone can accelerate your ability to both track and control your spending. It's so easy to buy things we really can't afford by just putting it on credit, and what starts off as a small balance soon becomes a large one, taking years to pay off purchases that have long since been consumed.

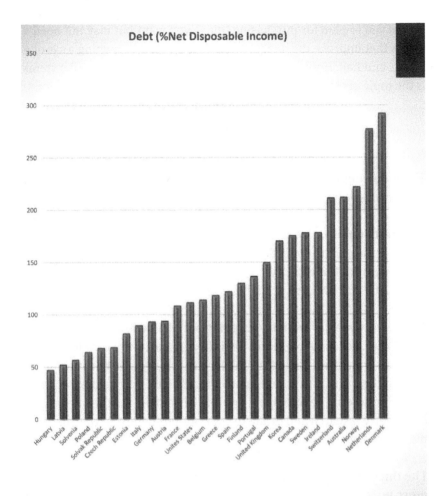

Household debt (Total, % of net disposable income, 2015)

Source: OECD, National Accounts at a Glance

PAYING FOR A COLLEGE EDUCATION

Most of us at some time face the challenge of paying for higher education, whether trying to find scholarships for ourselves or helping a loved one achieve their academic goals. Not only have educational standards greatly changed recently, but professions have become more specialized, meaning that students now need a higher degree – perhaps a master's degree or specialized training – just to land their first job.

As student loans are becoming more difficult to obtain, carefully planning to save for college has become crucial. Assuming the person going to college is not yet eighteen, these investments should be made in an Education Savings Account.

Table 4.1: *Worksheet for Financial Planning for Higher Education*

EXPECTED COST OF COLLEGE EDUCATION

SCHEDULE A: Expected Cost of College Education

		FATIMA	YOUR CHILD
1.	Current age of the child.	8	
2.	Years to college (18 minus child's age).	10	
3.	The current cost of a college education (in-state) (in 2011, approximately $6,000 per year).	$6,000	
4.	Inflation factor (from Table 4.2) corresponding to number of years in line 2 above.	1.34	
5.	Multiply line 3 by line 4 above to find the estimated future cost of college education at the end of the number of years specified in line 2.	$8,040	
6.	Future total cost for four years of college.	$32,160	

HOW MUCH SHOULD BE INVESTED

SCHEDULE B: Lump Sum Investment

		FATIMA	YOUR CHILD
1.	Enter amount from line 6 in Schedule A.	$32,160	
2.	Enter lump sum return factor from Table 4.3.	2.16	
3.	Divide line 1 by line 2 to find lump sum investment now.	$14,900	

SCHEDULE C: Periodic Investment

		FATIMA	YOUR CHILD
1.	Enter amount from line 6 in Schedule A.	$32,160	
2.	Enter periodic return factor from Table 4.3.	14.50	
3.	Divide line 1 by line 2 to find the annual target amount.	$2,220	
4.	Divide line 3 by 4 to find the quarterly target amount.	$555	
5.	Divide line 3 by 12 to find the monthly target amount.	$185	

Table 4.2: *Inflation Factor*

(Assuming that the cost is rising due to inflation at an average of 3 percent per year)

YEARS TO EXPENDITURE	INFLATION FACTOR	YEARS TO EXPENDITURE	INFLATION FACTOR
1	1.03	10	1.34
2	1.06	11	1.38
3	1.09	12	1.42
4	1.12	13	1.47
5	1.16	14	1.51
6	1.19	15	1.56
7	1.23	16	1.60
8	1.26	17	1.65
9	1.30	18	1.70

Table 4.3: *Investment Factor*

(Assuming a pretax average return of 8 percent per year)

YEARS TO EXPENDITURE	LUMP SUM	PERIODIC YEARLY	YEARS TO EXPENDITURE	LUMP SUM	PERIODIC YEARLY
1	1.08	1.00	10	2.16	14.50
2	1.17	2.08	11	2.33	16.66
3	1.26	3.25	12	2.51	18.99
4	1.36	4.51	13	2.71	21.51
5	1.47	5.87	14	2.92	24.23
6	1.59	7.34	15	3.15	27.16
7	1.72	8.92	16	3.40	30.33
8	1.86	10.64	17	3.67	33.75
9	2,00	12.50	18	3.96	37.45

Table 4.4: *Worksheet for Hajj Financial Planning*

EXPECTED COST OF HAJJ

SCHEDULE A: Cost of Hajj

1. Number of years from now when you plan to make hajj (*Insha Allah*). $ _____

2. The current cost of hajj per person (in 2011, about $5,000). $ _____

3. Enter inflation factor (from Table 4.2) corresponding to number of years in line 1 above. $ _____

4. Multiply line 2 by line 3 above to find the estimated future cost of hajj at the end of the numbers of years you specified in line 1. $ _____

HOW MUCH SHOULD BE INVESTED

SCHEDULE B: Lump Sum Investment

1. Enter amount from line 4 in Schedule A. $ _____

2. Enter lump sum return factor from Table 4.3. $ _____

3. Divide line 1 by line 2 to determine the lump sum investment required. $ _____

SCHEDULE C: Periodic Investment

1. Enter amount from line 4 in Schedule A. $ _____

2. Enter periodic return factor from Table 4.2. $ _____

3. Divide line 1 by line 2 to find the annual target amount. $ _____

4. Divide line 3 by 4 to find the quarterly target amount. $ _____

5. Divide line 3 by 12 to find the monthly target amount. $ _____

GIVING

**❝ HELP YOURSELF BY HELPING OTHERS.
THOSE WHO DO GOOD, DO WELL. ❞**
Sir John Templeton

GIVING IS THE ESSENCE OF LIVING.

GIVING is the essence of living. It touches everything we do that is truly meaningful. I believe we are all here to make a difference – otherwise what is the purpose of living? As we live and experience the world during our time here, our contributions hopefully leave the world a better place. We also give to provide cross-generational fairness; that is, if we are doing well, then let us do something so the next generation will have the same opportunities.

HOWEVER, BY SERVING THOSE GENUINELY IN NEED, WE ARE SERVING GOD HIMSELF.

Giving is not meant to encourage dependency in the receiver or create a permanent underclass. Most of us support the principle: it is better to teach a man how to fish than to give him a fish. However, by

serving those genuinely in need, we are serving God Himself. This is said on multiple occasions in the Qur'an as well as in the Jewish Bible and the Christian New Testament:

> And don't forget to do good and to share with those in need. These are the sacrifices that please God. (Hebrews 13:16)

> And spend of your substance in the cause of Allah, and make not your own hands contribute to (your) destruction; but do good; for Allah loves those who do good. (Q 2:195)

> Those who spend (in charity) of their goods by night and by day, in secret and in public, have their reward with their Lord: on them shall be no fear, nor shall they grieve. (Q 2:274)

> For I was hungry and you gave me something to eat, I was thirsty and you gave me something to drink, I was a stranger and you invited me in, I needed clothes and you clothed me, I was sick and you looked after me, I was in prison and you came to visit me. (Matthew 25:35–36)

> You will be made rich in every way so that you can be generous
> on every occasion. (2 Corinthians 9:11)

> You shall open your hand to your brother, to your poor and needy
> in your land. (Deuteronomy 15:11)

A person who cannot give money should give whatever they have
available to give, as illustrated in the following two stories:

> Prophet Muhammad said: "Every Muslim has to give in charity."
> The people then asked: "[But what] if someone has nothing to
> give, what should he do?" The Prophet replied: "He should work
> with his hands and benefit himself and also give in charity [from
> what he earns]." The people further asked: "If he cannot do
> [even] that?" The Prophet said finally: "Then he should perform
> good deeds and keep away from evil deeds, and that will be
> regarded as charitable deeds."[24]

> Prophet Muhammad said: "Charity is prescribed for each
> descendant of Adam every day the sun rises." He was then asked:
> "From what do we give charity every day?" The Prophet
> answered: "The doors of goodness are many ... enjoining good,
> forbidding evil, removing harm from the road, listening to the
> deaf, leading the blind, guiding one to the object of his need,
> hurrying with the strength of one's legs to one in sorrow who is
> asking for help, and supporting the feeble with the strength of
> one's arms – all of these are charity prescribed for you." He also
> said: "Your smile for your brother is charity."[25]

In Islam, giving falls into two categories: obligatory giving, called zakah,
and voluntary giving, known as ṣadaqah.

The Prophet said:

> God, whose Majesty and Glory are but manifest, has enjoined a

portion for the poor in the wealth of the rich that is within their capacity [to give]. If they withhold it from them until they go hungry, naked, or their lives become a continuous hardship, God shall be severe in holding them accountable for what they had done and punishment shall be stern (narrated by ʿAlī ibn Abī Ṭālib).

In light of the aforementioned statements, I often wonder about the significance of the various percentages of zakah ("portion" of wealth prescribed) on different sources of wealth – what do these various percentages really mean?

I recognize that many Muslims distribute their zakah directly to individuals or charitable organizations of their choice; therefore, estimating total zakah that is being given out (by a community as a whole) is nearly impossible.[26] However, I made a very rough estimate that faith-based community centers like those found among Muslim communities (and in the other Abrahamic faiths) often receive perhaps 10 percent of the zakah that is actually due of that community. But I am

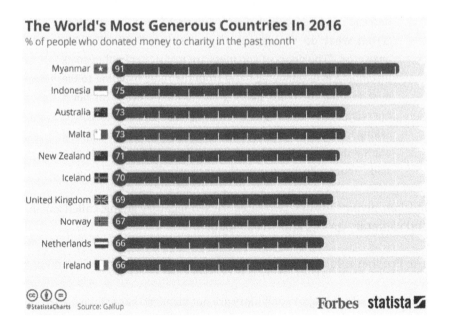

The World's Most Generous Countries In 2016
% of people who donated money to charity in the past month

Country	%
Myanmar	91
Indonesia	75
Australia	73
Malta	73
New Zealand	71
Iceland	70
United Kingdom	69
Norway	67
Netherlands	66
Ireland	66

@StatistaCharts   Source: Gallup

Forbes statista

an optimist at heart. I feel that, if every Muslim (and person of faith) calculates their zakah (tithe) accurately – based on the prescribed percentage(s) – and faithfully distributes it on a consistent basis, then we should be able to totally eliminate poverty from the world.

> ## IF YOU HAVE MUCH, GIVE OF YOUR WEALTH; IF YOU HAVE LITTLE, GIVE OF YOUR HEART.
> *ARABIC PROVERB*

If this was not to happen, the Creator might have chosen higher percentages, so that poverty would be eliminated and everyone would live with dignity! In fact, it has been historically documented that we once lived in a time when Muslims, when seeking to pay zakah, could not find anyone who qualified to receive the tithe.

UNDERSTANDING ZAKAH

For those who have money to give, Islamic law requires that they give it on a yearly basis as zakah (charity, or wealth tax). Zakah is considered so important that it is the third of the five pillars of Islamic faith.

Fulfillment of this pillar requires Muslims to reach out to the community and to interact with others in a meaningful and profound way. Just imagine, how would you know if someone is in debt? Is that person going to approach us and say, "I have $17,000 in credit card debt?" Probably not. However we may come to know this as we become actively involved in the community and exchanges of personal information occur. Then we can know who is in need of receiving zakah.

Zakah is similar to tithing in Jewish and Christian traditions. The words in Hebrew (ma'aser) and in Greek (apodekatoo) for "tithe" both simply mean "a tenth." The Hebrew Bible says one should tithe 10 percent of what one earns:

"For every tenth part of herd or flock, whatever passes under the rod, the tenth one shall be holy to the Lord." (Leviticus 27:33)

"and this stone that I have set up as a pillar will be God's house, and of all that you give me I will give you a tenth." (Genesis 28:22)

In the New Testament the actual percentage required is unclear. It simply suggests tithing "in keeping with your income" (I Corinthians). Some churches use the 10 percent figure stated in the Jewish scripture as a general guideline or "recommended minimum."

Calculating Zakah

Zakah is due on the current year's gross income before taxes – zakah, the right of Allah, is calculated before the rights of man (taxes).[27]

Zakah is also due on savings and investments that their owner has held for one lunar year, all stocks in trade above the *niṣāb*, and real estate and capital goods if they are owned (not kept on credit) and stocked for trade (not production).

Table 5.1: *Zakah Calculation Form*

SCHEDULE 1:
Items Subject to 2.58%* on Income and Assests

1. Any cash on hand kept for one Gregorian year. $_____

2. Annual earned income before any deductions of taxes, $_____
   social security, etc.

3. Value of jewelry kept for a year that is in excess of $_____
   what is customarily used.

   ADD LINES 1, 2, and 3. $_____

4. Less pro-rata *Nisab* (please see example below). $_____

5. Income subject to Zakah. $_____

6. Multiply line 5 by 2.58%. $_____

   SCHEDULE 1 ZAKAH DUE $_____

SCHEDULE 2:
Items Subject to 10.3%* Zakah on Yield

1. Realized capital gain on sales of stocks and mutual funds $_____
   and the like.

2. Dividends and rents from real estate, less expenses of debt $_____
   and any other direct expenses, but not depreciation or reserves
   or taxes.

3. The profits of shares in partnership, before deducting any $_____
   depreciation or reserves or taxes.

4. The net profit (revenue minus direct expenses such as wages, $_____
   maintenance, taxes, debts, etc. and not considering reserves)
   of trade, business or rented property.

   ADD LINES 1 through to 4. $_____

5. Less pro-rata *Nisab* (please see example below). $_____

6. Income subject to Zakah. $_____

7. Multiply line 6 by 10.3%. $_____

   SCHEDULE 2 ZAKAH DUE $_____

ZAKAH DUE (Add schedule 1 and 2).   TOTAL $_____

* Gregorian year is 11 days longer than lunar year; hence the adjusted rates are
  2.58% (rather than 2.5%) and 10.3% (rather than 10%) per year.

Table 5.1: *Continued*

REMARK: If the income subject to zakah is composed of items subject to 2.58% (schedule 1) and others whose yield is subject to 10.3% (schedule 2), nisab has to be divided in the same proportion of the two items. The nisab proportion is subtracted from each category, and the result is to be multiplied by the related rate, 2.58% or 10.3%.

EXAMPLE:

Total income from Schedule 1, subject to 2.58%	$50,000
Total income from Schedule 2, subject to 10.3%	$10,000
TOTAL YEARLY INCOME	$60,000

For a family/household size of 5

Nisab (Poverty Limit) = $27,000 to be divided into 22,500 and 4,500. Thus

Zakah on Schedule (1) = $50,000 - 22,500 = 27,500 x 2.58%	$710
Zakah on Schedule (2) = $10,000 - 4,500 = 5,500 x 10.3%	$567
TOTAL ZAKAH DUE	$1,277

Combined Zakah

Total Zakah (due for the year)	$ _____
Less Zakah already paid (during the year)	$ _____
ZAKAH DUE	$ _____

Hanafis say any delay in paying Zakah which is due (now owed to others), without valid reason, even for a day or two is sinful and not permitted.

Please send your tax-deductible Zakah contribution to:

FAITH
795 Center Street, Suite 2
Herndon, VA 20170 USA
www.faithus.org
Ph: (571) 323-2198

2012 Poverty Income Guidelines

HOUSEHOLD SIZE	ANNUAL INCOME Gregorian Year (up to)
1	11,170
2	15,130
3	19,090
4	23,050
5	27,000
6	30,970
7	34,930
8	38,890
9	42,850
10	46,810

Giving While Living

A man came to the Prophet and asked:

> "O Allah's Apostle! Which charity is the most superior in reward?" He replied, "The charity which you practice while you are healthy, niggardly [miserly] and afraid of poverty and wish to become wealthy. Do not delay it to the time of approaching death and then say, 'Give so much to such and such, and so much to such and such.' And it has already belonged to such and such [as it is too late]."[28]

Following this hadith, I strongly argue for giving while living. Why? Giving while living provides you with an opportunity to see the effects of your gift. While living, you can direct or redirect the use of your contributions. If a project you contributed to does not succeed, you have the opportunity to contribute to another one.

Abū Saʿīd al-Khudrī reported God's Messenger as saying, "It is better for a man to give a dirham as ṣadaqah (charity) during his lifetime, than to give a hundred at the time of his death."[29]

You may ask: "Is it better to leave for a child a trust account or a great society?"

ABŪ SAʿĪD AL-KHUDRĪ REPORTED GOD'S MESSENGER AS SAYING, "IT IS BETTER FOR A MAN TO GIVE A DIRHAM AS *ṢADAQAH* (CHARITY) DURING HIS LIFETIME, THAN TO GIVE A HUNDRED AT THE TIME OF HIS DEATH."

Vehicles for Giving While Living

KEY WEALTH-BUILDING & WEALTH-PRESERVING STRATEGIES

This section discusses some of the basic strategies for building and preserving the wealth you have earned, saved, and invested. These strategies can support and supplement your efforts with the five pillars of prosperity.

In building your financial future, a long-term, consistent approach is very important. Fundamental to this approach is determining your financial goals and charting out a plan to reach them. The following is an example of how to think through and establish financial goals. You can adapt this thinking to suit your own situation and goals.

IN BUILDING YOUR FINANCIAL FUTURE, A LONG-TERM, CONSISTENT APPROACH IS VERY IMPORTANT.

I want to use my wealth to do the following:
Buy a car
Buy a house
Put kids through college Go on pilgrimage (hajj) Buy a business
Retire comfortably
Help others

To accomplish these purposes my short-term goals are the following:

- Accumulate one year's worth of savings to go on pilgrimage
- Accumulate three years' worth of savings to purchase a car
- Accumulate five years' worth of savings for a down payment on a house

My long-term goals are the following:

- Accumulate $15,000 savings in eight years to help a child with college
- Accumulate twenty years' worth of savings for a comfortable retirement

My strategies for building wealth are the following:

- Save each month
- Budget to save and invest
- Invest and use compound returns
- Invest in a house
- Pay off any debt I have quickly
- Fully use tax-deferred investments: IRA, SEP-IRA, 401(K) plan, education IRA

My strategies for controlling debt are the following:

- Set debt-management goals
- Avoid accumulating debt

GROWING YOUR ASSETS

When you want to build a sizable estate, you should start early. In fact, you should start today. The sooner you invest, the sooner your money can start to grow.

You do not need a lot of money to start. Many mutual funds, including Amana Mutual Fund (www.amanafunds.com), allow you to start an account with as little as $250. You may also open a brokerage account if you have enough money to make investments of your choice. It is best to open an investment account that is separate from your checking and savings accounts. This allows you to follow your investment money and also reduces the temptation to spend it.

There are two great ways to invest. One way is to buy things of value whose value you expect to increase over time, such as real estate, stocks, art, or collectibles (a growth investment). Another way is to buy things that you expect will provide regular income, for example, in the form of rents or dividends.

THERE ARE TWO GREAT WAYS TO INVEST. ONE WAY IS TO BUY THINGS OF VALUE WHOSE VALUE YOU EXPECT TO INCREASE OVER TIME, SUCH AS REAL ESTATE, STOCKS, ART, OR COLLECTIBLES (A GROWTH INVESTMENT). ANOTHER WAY IS TO BUY THINGS THAT YOU EXPECT WILL PROVIDE REGULAR INCOME, FOR EXAMPLE, IN THE FORM OF RENTS OR DIVIDENDS.

CONCLUSION

It is my hope that the ideas in this book, applied correctly, will help you to manage your finances wisely. This guide covers a few financial and moral principles that can provide you with spiritual fulfillment and economic success. When you earn, save, invest, spend, and give based on the advice outlined in this guide, you can live debt free, with your assets protected, and be taxed fairly. Also, your family's needs will be taken care of both now and in the future.

The ideas contained within this guide are based on my experience. Now you may benefit from them, or even improve upon them. If you have found this guide useful, please pray for me and just like me, make a donation to your favorite charity.

I'd like to end with the following hadith and a verse:

> The Prophet said: "O Allah! I seek refuge with You from worry and grief, I seek refuge with You from weakness and laziness, I seek refuge with You from cowardice and miserliness, and I seek refuge with You from being heavily in debt and from being overpowered by [other] men."

> Our Lord! Accept (this service) from us: for You are the All-Hearing, the All-Knowing. (Q. 2:127)

NOTES

1   Shaykh Yusuf Talal DeLorenzo, "Preface" in Virginia Morris and Brian D. Ingram, *Guide to Understanding Islamic Investing in Accordance with Islamic Shariah* (New York: Lightbulb Press, 2001), p.3.

2   Lynnette Khalfani-Cox, *Zero Debt – The Ultimate Guide to Financial Freedom* (New Jersey: Advantage World Press, 2004), p.8.

3   *Sahih al-Bukhari* 2:292, cited in Irfan Ul Haq, *Economic Doctrines of Islam*, p.114.

4   Hadith of the Prohet Muhammad, reported by Abu Daoud.

5   Hadith, reported by al-Nisai and al-Hakim.

6   Hadith, reported by Muslim.

7   Portions of this chapter reference Yusuf al-Qaradawi, *Halal and Haram in Islam* (Indianapolis, IN: American Trust Publications, 1987), pp. 268-269, concerning the Prophet seeking refuge with God from debt.

8   M. Umer Chapra, *Towards a Just Monetary System: A Discussion of Money, Banking and Monetary Policy in the Light of Islamic Teachings* (London: The Islamic Foundation, 1995).

9   Morris and Ingram, *Guide to Understanding Islamic Investing*, p.10.

10   Excerpted from Jerald F. Dirks, *The Abrahamic Faiths: Judaism, Christianity, and Islam: Similarities and Contrasts* (Beltsville, MD: Amana Publications, 2004), p.29.

11   William W. Baker, *More In Common Than You Think: The Bridge Between Islam and Christianity* (Crane, MO: Defender Publications, 1998).

12   "Oneness of Humanity," Los Angeles Chinese Learning Center, http://chinese-school.netfirms.com/Judaism-Christianity-Islam.html.

13   Muhammad Ali al-Hashimi, *The Ideal Muslim Society as Defined in the Qur'an and Sunnah* (Riyadh, Saudi Arabia: International Islamic Publishing House, 2010), p. 180.

14   Al-Hashimi, *Ideal Muslim Society*, p. 180 (taken from Hadith as recorded by

Bukhari and Muslim).

15 Ibid, p. 419.

16 Hadith narrated by Tabarani and al-Bazzar.

17 Ibrahim Abdul-Matin, *Green Deen: What Islam Teaches about Protecting the Planet* (San Francisco: Berrett-Koehler Publishers, 2010).

18 Remarks from a discussion I had with Joseph Montville, Chair, Center for World Religions, Diplomacy, and Conflict Resolution, George Mason University.

19 Adapted from Ul Haq, *Economic Doctrines of Islam*, pp. 92-93.

20 The Fairfax Institute, located in Herndon, Virginia, offers a course on faith-based entrepreneurship. Those interested in pursuing and/or exploring entrepreneurship are encouraged to take this course. For more information on the course, contact the Institute at https://www.thefairfaxinstitute.org.

21 Warren Buffet and Lawrence Cunningham, *The Essays of Warren Buffet: Lessons for Corporate America* (New York: The Cunningham Group, 2008).

22 Starbucks Investor Relations, *Financial Release* (Seattle: Starbucks Coffee Company, 2011).

23 Ul Haq, *Economic Doctrines of Islam*, p. 158.

24 *Sahih al-Bukhari*, Volume 2, Hadith 524.

25 *Fiqh-us-Sunnah*, Volume 3, Number 98.

26 Vijay Mahajan, *The Arab World Unbound* (San Francisco: Jossey-Bass, 2009), p.108.

27 Abu-Saud, M., *Contemporary Zakat*, p. 164.

28 Bukhari, Book 2 (vol. 24), hadith 500.

29 *Readings on Charity and Kindness in Islam* (Plainfield, IN: ISNA Development Foundation, 2002), p.19.

BIBLIOGRAPHY

Abdul-Matin, Ibrahim. *Green Deen: What Islam Teaches about Protecting the Planet* (San Francisco: Berrett-Koehler Publishers, 2010).

Abu Saud, Mahmoud. *Contemporary Zakah* (Cincinnati, OH: Zakat and Research Foundation, 1988).

Ackerman, Ruthie. "God's My Investment Advisor: Faith-Based Funds Doing Well." *American Banker* (December 21, 2009).

Baker, William W. *More In Common Than You Think: The Bridge Between Islam and Christianity* (Crane, MO: Defendant Publications, 1998).

Buffet, Warren and Lawerence Cunningham. *The Essays of Warren Buffet: Lessons for Corporate America* (New York: The Cunningham Group, 2008).

Chapra, M. Umer. *Islam and the Economic Challenge* (Nairobi: The Islamic Foundation, 1982). *Towards a Just Monetary System: A Discussion of Money, Banking and Monetary Policy in the Light of Islamic Teachings* (London: The Islamic Foundation, 1995).

Khalfani-Cox, Lynnette. *Zero Debt – The Ultimate Guide to Financial Freedom* (South Orange, NJ: Advantage World Press, 2004).

Davis, John E. *Shared Equity Homeownership: The Changing Landscape of Resale-Restricted Owner-Occupied Housing* (Montclair, NJ: National Housing Institute, 2006).

DeLorenzo, Shaykh Yusuf Talal. "Preface" in Virginia Morris and Brian D. Ingram, *Guide to Understanding Islamic Investing in Accordance with Islamic Shariah* (New York: Lightbulb Press, 2001).

Dirks, Jerald F. *The Abrahamic Faiths: Judaism, Christianity, and Islam: Similarities and Contrasts* (Beltsville, MD: Amana Publications, 2004).

El Diwany, Tarek (ed.). *Islamic Banking and Finance: What It Is and What It Could Be* (London: 1st Ethical Charitable Trust, U.K, 2010).

DuLong, Jessica. "The Imam of Bedford-Stuyvesant." *Aramco World* (May-June 2005).

Elnadav, Shaul. "Estate Planning, Halacha and the Jewish Law of Inheritance." *Jewish Legal Perspectives* (January 15, 2010). http://jlperspectives.org/2010/01/15/estate-planning-halacha-and-the-jewish-law-of-inheritance/

Ferruelo, Elizabeth. "Why Socially Responsible Investing and Islamic Finance is on the Rise." Forbes.com, November 1, 2012. http://www.forbes.com/sites/ashoka/2012/11/01/why-there-is-high-growth-potential-in-the-nexus-between-socially-responsible-investing-and-islamic-finance/.

Fisher, Omar Clark. *Islamic Wealth Guide: Guide to Wealth Building, Risk Management and Wealth Distribution in Accordance with Islamic Shariah* (Oakton, VA: self published, 2007).

Grudem, Wayne. *Business for the Glory of God: The Bible's Teaching on the Moral Goodness of Business* (Wheaton, IL: Crossway Books, 2003).

_____."How Business in Itself Can Glorify God" in Tetsunao Yamamori and Kenneth Eldred, *On Kingdom Business: Transforming Missions through Entrepreneurial Strategies* (Wheaton, IL: Crossway Books, 2003).

Haq, Irfan Ul. *Economic Doctrines of Islam: A Study in the Doctrines of Islam and Their Implications for Poverty, Employment and Economic Growth* (Herndon, Va.: International Institute of Islamic Thought, 1996).

al-Hashimi, Muhammad Ali. *The Ideal Muslim Society as Defined in the Qur'an and Sunnah* (Riyadh, Saudi Arabia: International Islamic Publishing House, 2010).

Kamali, Mohammad Hashim. *Maqasid Al-Shariah: Ijtihad and Civilizational Renewal* (London: The International Institute of Islamic Thought, 2012).

Khan, Muhammad Muhsin. *Summarized Sahih al Bukkari* (Riyadh, Saudi Arabia: Darussalam 1996).

Mahajan, Vijay. *The Arab World Unbound* (San Francisco: Jossey-Bass, 2009).

Mauboussin, Michael. "Why Smart People Make Dumb Decisions." *The Futurist* 44:2 (March 6, 2010).

Moore, Gary A. *Faithful Finances 101: From Poverty of Fear and Greed to the Riches of Spiritual Investing* (Radnor, PA: Templeton Press, 2005).

Morris, Virginia. *A Muslim's Guide to Investing and Personal Finance* (New York: Lighthouse Press, 2009).

Morris, Virginia and Brian D. Ingram. *Guide to Understanding Islamic Investing in Accordance with Islamic Shariah* (New York: Lightbulb Press, 2001).

Al-Mubarakpuri, Shaykh Safiur Rahman. *Tafsir Ibn Kathir*, Vol. 4. (Riyad:

Maktaba Dar-us-Salam, 2003).

Nass, Herbert. *The 101 Biggest Estate Planning Mistakes* (Hoboken, NJ: John Wiley and Sons, 2010).

Nichols, Dwight. *God's Plans for Your Finances* (New Kensington, PA: Whitaker House, 1998).

Only for the Love of Allah by Night and by Day: Readings on Charity and Kindness in Islam (Plainfield, IN: ISNA Development Foundation, 2002).

Orman, Suze. *The 9 Steps to Financial Freedom: Practical and Spiritual Steps So You Can Stop Worrying* (New York: Three Rivers Press, 2006).

Osman, Fathi. *Concepts of the Quran* (Los Angeles: MVI Publications, 1997).

Owens, Stephen. "Biblical Entrepreneurship: The Purpose of a Christian Entrepreneur." *Ezine Articles.* http://ezinearticles.com/?Biblical-Entrepreneurship—-The-Purpose-of-a-Christian-Entrepreneur&id=1222706

al-Qaradawi, Yusuf. *Halal and Haram in Islam* (Indianapolis, IN: American Trust Publications, 1987.)

_____. *Fiqh al-Zakah: A Comparative Study* (London: Dar al-Taqwa,1999).

Quilla, Oliver. "Warren Buffett, "The Billionaire Next Door." May 7, 2007. http://www.cnbc.com/id/17595710.

Scottrade. *2011 American Retirement Survey* (St. Louis: Scottrade, 2011).

Sethi, Ramit. *I Will Teach You to Be Rich* (New York: Workman, 2009).

Siddiqi, Muhammad N. *Economic Enterprise in Islam* (Lahore: Islamic Publications, 1972).

Singletary, Michelle. *7 Money Mantras for a Richer Life: How to Live Well with the Money You Have* (New York: Random House, 2003).

Soaries, Deforest. "Debt-free Living is the Key to Power." CNN article date 11/14/2010. http://www.cnn.com/2010/OPINION/10/17/inam.soaries.dfree.pulpit/index.html

St. Marie, Geoffrey. "Christian Inheritance Law." *EHow.Com.* www.ehow.com/facts_6831123/Christian-inheritance-law.html

Starbuck Investor Relations. *Financial Release* (Seattle, Washington: Starbucks Coffee Company, 2011).

Usmani, Mufti Muhammad Taqi. "Looking for New Steps in Islamic Finance." www.muftitaqiusmani.com.

ABOUT THE AUTHOR

DR. M. YAQUB MIRZA is President and Chief Executive Officer of Sterling Management Group, Inc. Sterling negotiates mergers, acquisitions, and sales of various-sized companies located in different parts of the world. Sterling and its affiliates operate in the United States, Canada, Chile, Egypt, Malaysia, Turkey, and Zimbabwe. In addition, Dr. Mirza has more than thirty years of experience in stock investments and portfolio management.

Dr. Mirza serves as the Chairman of the Board of Trustees of Amana Mutual Funds, (Assets $3.3 billion) which is registered with the Securities and Exchange Commission. He also serves on the boards of numerous other organizations, including several for-profit and not-for-profit, as well as academic institutions.

Dr. Mirza is a member of the Board of Advisors for the College of Humanities and Social Sciences, George Mason University in Fairfax, Virginia, and the Board of Advisors, Byrd School of Business, Shenandoah University, Winchester, Virginia. He is a Trustee on the George Mason University Foundation. He is also a member of the Board of Trustees of Shenandoah University. In addition, he is a member of the Finance Committee (budget of about $100 million) and Investment and Endowment Committee of Shenandoah University.

Dr. Mirza has received numerous awards and much recognition for his work in entrepreneurship and community service, including the 2002 Entrepreneur Award by the Islamic Chamber of Commerce and Industry (San Jose, California); 2006 Award Recipient – Byrd Distinguished Entrepreneur Speaker Series, Byrd School of Business at Shenandoah University; 2012 Recognition Award for Community Service by the American Muslim Alliance; 2013 Award from the Muslim American Coalition Council and Public Affairs Council and the ISNA

Community Service Award 2015. Most notably, Dr. Mirza was featured in an article on faith-based entrepreneurship, published in the 2010 spring edition of the *New England Journal of Entrepreneurship*.

Dr. Mirza holds a MSc from the University of Karachi (1969), a PhD in Physics (1974) and an MA in Teaching Science (1975) from the University of Texas at Dallas.